dear me,

IT WASN'T YOUR FAULT;
BELIEVE ME THIS TIME

TRIGGER WARNING:
MENTAL ILLNESS, SELF-HARM, SUICIDE

Dear Me, It Wasn't Your Fault; Believe Me This Time

Copyright @ 2023
Jetlyn Nobes

YGTMedia Co. Press Trade Paperback Edition

Published in Canada, for Global Distribution
by YGTMedia Co.

www.ygtmedia.co/publishing

ISBN 978-1-998754-26-7

Printed in North America

dear me,

IT WASN'T YOUR FAULT; BELIEVE ME THIS TIME

Jetlyn Nobes

To my younger self,
Whom I did not love enough;
and to others out there
learning to love themselves

Contents

The Falling
-01-

The Crashing
-27-

The Landing
-55-

The Final Destination
-83-

The
Falling

I'm writing this as I go through my journey

And I want you to know
it'll be okay one day

You will heal
You will find yourself
You will be able to live
You will be happy

But most of all
You're going to fall in love again
but this time
with yourself

Jetty,

Compete with . . .

A smile on your face,

A smile in your heart,

And fire in your belly.

Believe in yourself; you will be great.

Love, Dad

And just like that, this was the last letter

I'd ever get from you

Okay, truth is,
I have no idea what I'm doing
or where to start

I don't even know why I'm still alive
but I am

And I guess
I'll have to stick around a bit longer to finish this . . .
and so will you

I remember the first time you held my hand
I remember our first hug
I remember our first Daddy–Daughter dance

I remember the first time you taught me
how to skate
I remember you

I am trying to remember remembering you and
I cannot seem to remember as much anymore
I cannot remember your voice by heart
and
I cannot remember how your hugs felt

What I do remember and seem to only remember
are memories . . .
The good ones
The laughs, the dances, how amazing you were,
and
our karaoke nights

(continued)

But I also remember
the last time I hugged you
I remember the last time I saw you
The last time I laid my eyes on you:
But you weren't there
You were on a stretcher
I couldn't see your face
but I saw your body in a bag
and that's when I knew
it was the first last time seeing you
and I cannot not remember that

It's silly, isn't it?
Most people write books about their journey
after getting through it
after finding hope

But me

There's none
I lost all hope for myself

My depression is caving me in
Inside this deep hole
I no longer think I'll be able to climb out of

I am trapped
I am alone
I am scared

Where am I?
Who am I?

I am gone

Fuck you, mental illnesses

For taking away
my father
my best friend
the first man who ever loved me

He was supposed to walk me down the aisle
He was supposed to be here my whole life

But he's not
Well, at least not anymore

Because of you
I should've known you were taking over him

I'm sorry, Dad
I tried my best to save you

I used to think you left me because
I wasn't a good-enough daughter
or I was too difficult and never understood why

But now I know
You were already gone
Lost, taken over by your brain

I wish you would've left some sort of letter
or something to help me understand
I was only twelve

But I promise you
I'm not mad, I understand now
I just want you back

I like to believe you're in heaven

I think I only do that because it makes me find
some sort of peace with your death

But the truth is,
I'm just scared to think
that you are no longer a thing

That you are just completely dead, nothing, gone
and never coming back

And that terrifies me most

I'm slowly falling back
into the dark tunnel
I fought incredibly hard to get out of the last time

I have disgusting red marks
all over me

I hate them, I say
but I still make them

Why?

Your skin is not paper
Or an apple

DO NOT cut yourself
because you feel like you deserve it

I'm here, I'm listening, and I'm telling you
It's not worth it

You kept me alive
on days I could barely hold on

You opened my heart
on days I was isolated in my mind

You gave me purpose
You are my purpose

And because of you, I found mine

I hope you find yours too someday . . .

We're told to stay close to people who feel
like sunlight,
but you are far more than just that,
you are the whole sunrise to my life

Adore your body

When nobody else will be there for you,
It will be

It's not a punishment to be so empathetic,
it's a gift (somebody once told me)

Use it

But beware that
it doesn't bring you down to a dark place
like it did with me

Why do people who want to live
end up dying with no choice

But

The ones who aren't physically sick
Want to end their lives?
People ask.

Well,
They are mentally sick,
they did not choose that life
or to be depressed
or to hear voices saying, "cut yourself"

And I know I didn't choose to take those pills . . .
Well, I did
But I didn't want to have this life
I didn't choose to want to kill myself
I just chose to do it
I didn't choose to be home when you died

(continued)

I went from choosing what I'd wear to the first
day of school
whether I'd wear my bright orange shirt with my
bright pink shorts
to choosing which dress to wear to your funeral

In less than a day,
I went from being a child to a grown-up

Be careful who you are kind to

You're not a road

You shouldn't be walked all over

Yet you can still choose to be kind

You don't really know what it feels like
even when you try
until it happens to you

I had a friend who lost her dad
and I didn't know how to help her or what to do
and I for sure did not know how badly it hurt her

Until I called 911
Until I ran out of the house and next door
to get help
Until I tried breaking open your door
Until a policewoman came out of our
caution-taped house bawling her eyes out
Until I watched them carry you out in a body bag
Until I watched people watch me cry at your
funeral

(continued)

Then I knew
I knew in that very moment that you were gone
I knew that it was never going to be the same
And I knew how much hurting there was for her

And I now know what it feels like
When it happens to you

I care so much about everyone else
but still so little about myself

Why do I hate myself so much?
It's time to go, Jetty

Am I hard to love?
NO
YOU
ARE
NOT
You are just too kind
to people who don't deserve it, love

You have so much love in your heart
Don't waste it on people
who aren't worthy of receiving it

Use some on yourself
You're important too

You shouldn't be crying thunderstorms
over somebody who decided to be the raincloud

Dear Me,

I will not let you treat that twelve-year-old girl
like that
I won't let you blame her anymore
or tear her into pieces
or call her names
I will not let you cut her skin
because she thinks she deserves it
She's still a little girl

–Me, Myself, and I

The
Crashing

I'm not telling you all this because
I want you to feel bad
or have sympathy for me
Because honestly, I couldn't care less if you care
or not

Instead, I'm telling you all this because
I want you to know, you can go through so much
and still be alive in the end

You can think your world is ending
and still be able to smile

I want you always to be kind to others
because you just never know what's going on in
somebody's mind

The first time I discovered
I could make marks on my body
I was thirteen
I remember being so excited to be home alone
because it meant
I could feel the silver blade
slipping through my skin
like my body was being filled
by fires everywhere

I was still so young

I continued doing it
Every day
Every night
Every day
Every night
Until I couldn't feel it anymore

It was an obsession . . .
An addiction
I couldn't stop

Everyone has a page in their life
they choose to not read aloud

You have not a clue in the world
What others go through

I was around seven
when I was bullied for the first time

And I thought I was just disgusting
That's why she locked me in another room

But really, she just didn't like me, I guess
I was three years younger

You were supposed to be a big sister to me

When I was nine
I started doing these weird facial movements that
I could not control
Everyone would laugh at me
or ask me why I did them

But I didn't know

I didn't want to twist my eyes that way
then have to turn my wrists ten times a second
and rotate my neck every minute
But it was a part of me that I couldn't change
and I eventually had to accept that

When I was nine
I started getting terribly painful stomachaches
to the point where I couldn't move
all because of anxiety
I was only nine

When I was ten
the doctor told me I had tics,
and I didn't want to be alive anymore
It was tiring for a ten-year-old

It turns out they were just anxiety tics
but they still haven't gone away
I remember trying to force myself
not to do them
so people didn't look at me weirdly
I was the puppeteer to my own body

When I turned eleven
I started having to step with a certain leg first
I had to say something five times because
something was telling me I needed to
I remember having to turn the shower knob with
both hands
or else something would happen to my family
But it wasn't that bad till I turned thirteen

When I was twelve

I was home with my siblings

when my dad passed away

We found out he'd had a brain disease

that led him to do it

I wish I hadn't been home

When I was thirteen
I moved to a different province
I had gotten into a draining relationship
and was getting touched in places
I didn't want to be
by someone

When I was fourteen
I was in one of the darkest places I'd ever been
in the short years of my life

I was scared
I was gone
I was terrified

My stomach pain started getting worse
I remember having to call my mom at night
and barfing all over my bed because of how
much it hurt

And the anxiety got bad
I wasn't in control;
I was completely and utterly
Lost

March 6
I think was the darkest day of my life

No

It *was* the darkest day
I woke up
and took a bath

A few hours later
I found myself lying in an ambulance
because I'd taken too many "happy pills"

Oh, Mom
I'm so sorry
I'm sorry you had to be home, Darc

The doctors asked me if it was a plan . . .
At the time I said no
because I just wanted to go home

But it was a lie; I knew what I was doing
If I'd been honest
would I be okay now?

Today is my fifteenth birthday,
and if I'm going to be honest
I never thought I'd make it past fourteen

I thought I might feel some happiness today
because it's the day I came to life . . .
A day all about me

But I still feel so broken

And the saddest thing is, last night
I didn't think I'd make it to my birthday
But here I am

Everyone is telling me
I should be so proud
because I'm here
and I almost didn't make it

But I'm not

I wish I weren't here
I wished it had worked

But part of me just wishes
I could be proud of myself for once . . .

This is not a story of a girl's life,
it's the journey of one's pain
It's a book to help you get up in the morning and
realize your worth

It's to show you that
you are capable of having a life
You are capable of being what you want to be

It's the journey of one's grief, healing, and loving
themself
It's the journey of growing, finding, and planting
new seeds from their own dying flowers

I admire the people who can
get up and go on with their lives
even if they're struggling

I also admire people who can't always get up,
because look!
They're still here
and that . . .
that is just incredible

I'm those people
Just because the flowers may be dying
or
have been stepped on by muddy dogs
doesn't make them any less beautiful
than those shining bright in the garden

Actually

I find them quite pure
Not because I feel bad for them
but because
no matter how much they've been stepped on
they're still here

The most powerful piece of vocabulary
to ever come out of someone's mouth
is the word
help . . .
Yet nobody really says it.

Why?

Please, if you are out there
alone and struggling,
use the word
because I promise you
it will be worth it

Even in this very moment
if you feel like you have a thousand people all
over you
You will get through it

Okay?

I remember a time when I was really in a dark place
I watched a movie where a guy wrote stuff on sticky notes and put them on his wall

Well,
I decided to do that

On my wall, next to my bed
I have plenty of sticky notes
with daily affirmations and sayings on them
I know it sounds silly
but it helps
I promise you

Right in the heart of them all
I have a sticky note with one word on it:
Live
And every day I get up
I try to go through with it
and ever since then, I have

okay

okay

okay

okay

It's okay to just feel okay sometimes

Everybody wants a person
Wants to fall in love

I think it's silly

The truth is,
You find your soulmate,
when you start falling in love with yourself

You are your own person
Before you're anyone else's

Please do not let your body bleed
Please do not harm yourself
Please be gentle with your body

It's not meant to be broken
It's meant to help you live

I find it quite unbelievable
the pain people carry inside their hearts
for so long but don't tell anyone

It's like flowers:
You're not really aware
when they're dying
and need to be watered
until it's too late to save them

So please be impeccably good to people . . .
The world is too awful to be cruel

Dear thoughts,
I won't let you own me anymore
I won't let you shove me in a box

I won't let you tell me what to do
as if I'm your slave
I own you
You are not my heart
nor are you me
You are just my thoughts

You don't get to duct tape my mouth shut
or silence me anymore

Let me find myself again
Please
I'm begging you

A few months ago
I started taking an adaptive course
That teaches kids with special needs how to
cook, measure, and slice food
I was nervous at first
I had never really done anything like it before

But

That course saved my life
It taught me how much life is worth living
It taught me how to only see the good in the
world
and how effective the littlest things are

Not a single person in that room
full of thirty people (at least)
was judgmental
Not a single kid in that class
cared what you looked like or talked like or did

I really think those kids are the most beautiful
people in this world

To my partner in that class,

Thank you
Thank you for teaching me how to see a different
view of this world
Thank you for teaching me how to only see the
good in things
Thank you for showing me my purpose

I remember that time when I gave you a little
pouch of fidget toys
and you had pure joy on your face
playing with them

Right then and there
is when I changed

When I decided to see the good
in the littlest things
When I decided from now on I will choose to live

You came into my life
and taught me not only how beautiful the world is
but also how amazing YOU are

Thank you, A

To my second partner in that class,

Thank you
Thank you for loving me
when I felt lost in my mind
Thank you for never failing to make me smile
when I went to school
Mostly, thank you for teaching me
how to love myself

I met you at a time when I felt there was no way
out of my darkness
and
you brought me into your own light

You are the most beautiful human in the world
You are my favorite human
Most of all, you are my hero

Thank you, L

To my teacher in that class,

Thank you
Thank you for making me feel seen when I felt
like I was a ghost to the world
Thank you for never failing to make me feel
appreciated
Thank you for being the figure in my life I needed

I remember the time you told me I had a gift
I remember how you told me to keep going when
I thought I couldn't do it anymore
I didn't believe you because I saw myself as a
failure,
but now I do
I've realized because of you maybe my purpose
in this world
is not to try so hard to be liked by everyone
but
to try so hard to help others
because that's the gift you give as well

You helped me become me
You helped me love myself
You helped me through my darkness
Mostly, you helped me live

Thank you, Brown

The Landing

My OCD is enclosing me
in a world where I don't belong
It is controlling me
It is making me feel insane . . .
Am I crazy?

Touch this
Do this
Turn it this many times
Wrong, do it again

Cut yourself
Die
Die
Die
Die
Stop, please
I'm tired of you

I never told you
How badly you hurt me
How badly you broke me
Till there wasn't even a me anymore
My soul was not meant to be dug into like that
And my body was not meant to be exposed
this young

If you're reading this
I'm telling you now
You broke my soul
Until I couldn't look at anyone
without being scared

I used to think it was me
and I never forgave myself for that
But now
I forgive me
But I also
Forgive you

I think the reason we didn't work
was not because we didn't try
but because I fell more in love
with you
than myself

I lost myself trying to love you
and I don't mean
that I'm mad at you for that
but more so the fact that
I cannot love myself; it burns my soul

I think one of the most painful moments
after I tried committing
was when I was with my whole family at the
cottage
and everyone was singing and dancing
to "Piano Man"
I remember feeling this heart-sinking feeling
All I could think about was how I tried to leave
them;
how I wouldn't be able to see them again
I wondered if they would miss me
How it would feel

But the strongest thing I was thinking of
was you
I remember just wanting to be with you
Just wanting to visit you

And there it was:
the ending
I wanted so badly to just be dead
But there was always something
holding me back
another part of me kicking in
I think I saved myself from myself

That's not how it's going to end

Well, I think so, at least

I'm not going lie to you
and say one day you'll be okay
and to just give it time
because I hated when people said that to me

So instead
I'm going to say

You'll get through this
because you know what?
You woke up today and
you could have kept sleeping
But you opened your eyes
and that's just enough

Everyone works so hard
to be extraordinary their whole life
To do extraordinary things
To get extraordinary things

But the truth is, just being yourself,
an ordinary human,
is much more than
being an extraordinary person
So stop trying to be something you're not
because trust me,
you're far more perfect being yourself than
anyone else

I can remember the very first time
I felt lonely in a crowd of people

It was loud
There was music, dancing
My family
But not my father

It got hard when you left, Dad
I was only twelve

The little girl home alone
afraid because her dad had left
didn't deserve that

She used to be filled with joy and happiness
She only saw the good in the world
Where did she go?
I lost her

She grew up too fast
her heart not ready for that type of pain
She still blames herself for what happened
but, hon, it was not your fault

–Little Me

Dad, this one's for you
I'm sorry your brain was taken over
I wish I could have at least one more moment
with you
You were the best, most amazing dad

I'm so lucky I got to spend those twelve years
with you
You taught me how to be so strong

I know you can't read this because you're gone
But I hope you know
I'd rather only have had twelve years with you
than a lifetime with any other dad

I miss you

I miss you
more than I thought I could ever miss somebody

I never thought I could miss someone so much
It feels like my heart is shattered on the floor
and no one can ever piece it back together

Like my body is no longer me
because I died with you
Like I am just floating around watching
everybody live
Like I'm literally fucking broken

To be honest, I don't really know
who I am anymore
but at the same time, I do

I know that I'm strong and
I can get through anything
but at the same time, I'm weak
and the next little thing that comes
could break me

I know I can get through things on my own
because that's what I've always done
but the last time I tried that
I found myself almost dead

I don't recommend trying to get through things
alone
Everyone, at least sometimes, needs a pat on the
back
Someone saying they're proud of them
or someone to have, to talk to, and to be there
when there is no one else

But the truth is, there's always YOU
You're always going to be there for yourself
You really have no choice

The twelve-year-old little girl
didn't deserve that
She used to be filled with glitter and sunshine
She saw the good in everyone

Where did she go?
She had to grow up too fast
I lost her
Her little heart wasn't ready for that type of
burning pain
Now she's fifteen and still blames herself for the
death of her father

Dear Me,
It wasn't your fault;
Believe me this time

Home became a person when
I met a girl on my journey
Her heart was hurting, but she still tried to take
care of mine
At times she was awful to me
but it's just because she was fighting demons
in her brain

I'm glad to say that I am now learning to love her
She is worthy of me loving her
and deserves to be happy
I'm glad I found you, my home, myself

Experiment:
Count how many people leave you

One too many

My best friend in grade 8 and half of grade 9
was my favorite person of all time
until, you know, we just weren't meant to be
friends
But she used to write me little notes
at least once a week

And in one note, she said,
"I want you to know that you are strong, and I
know this because the strongest people are not
those who show strength in front of the world,
but those who fight and win battles that others
know nothing about."

I remember reading it and tearing up
Not because it was sad but because
for the first time, I had a person
I had somebody who told me I was special
But most of all, somebody who appreciated me
Somebody who saw me
Somebody who did not make me feel like a
nobody
Somebody who made me realize that I'm capable
of living

(continued)

And for that, I thank you
I thank you for being kind to me when I had
no one
and for loving me through my darkest times
I thank you for bandaging my wounds
and for holding onto them for the times
I could not hold them myself
Just know I'm not mad that we are now strangers
I'm just glad the next person you heal for a little
while gets to have you

I know you don't want to hurt others
when you leave
I know it makes you feel guilty, but please stay
At least just a while longer

It's not going to be a fast recovery
Boom, one day you're happy

It will take time, lots of time
It will be a struggle, it will hurt so bad
to the point you feel like you're never going
to get better

But what does better actually mean?
How do you know you're better?
You don't
You just get so used to feeling hurt that
when you do feel a bit of happiness you
push it away

But don't; let yourself have a laugh some days
Let yourself be okay sometimes

I'm not better right now
but I'm learning to let myself be happy
and not feel guilty about it

Life can be a bullet to the heart sometimes
But you know
you are strong

And if you're out there feeling like you need to die
because it's hurting so much
you will get through these tough times
Your time hasn't come yet
Keep fighting

And when the time comes when you feel
like you have no one
remember that I am proud of you
Remember that there's always somebody
out there
who looks at you and says,
"Wow, they can go through all that and still be
able to open their eyes in the morning"

There are little kids out there who stare at you
and think you look like a goddess
Just know, even when you feel like the world
hates you
there is always going to be somebody who
loves you

I promise you that

I'm sorry to all the people I hurt because I was
hurting
I'm sorry for all the times I cancelled right before
we hung out
It's not because of you
It was because my depression and anxiety
closed me in
and I just had no energy

I'm sorry to all the people I broke when I chose
not to live
I'm sorry to myself for all the times
I broke your heart
for all the times I called you names
mostly, for all the times I made you bleed
I hope you all forgive me some day

I know you are tired
I know you feel alone
and you're suffering
But, love,
you're a hero
You're incredibly captivating
So please keep breathing

Nothing is more powerful

than a person struggling

and

admitting they need help

and accepting it

And just by that

they are changing

not just their own, but many other people's lives

I am numb

The Final Destination

I suffer from mental illnesses
I never thought I'd have

But I am not embarrassed about them anymore
I don't feel like I need to hide them anymore

Most of all, I don't feel like they define me

You are not what you go through
But what you go through makes you who you are

I feel like lately I've been a cloud:
Not those white fluffy ones that show up
when there's sun
and not the ones that are crying so hard
their tears fall from the sky

I've just been a dark, dark cloud that stays there
not crying, but not bright
The dark cloud represents my numbness
cold and empty

I cannot seem to smile, but I cannot cry
I'm just here, existing
like another dark cloud in the sky
waiting for its turn to live

When I go into one of my
really bad depression periods
especially in September

I leave everyone
I stop trying
I believe there's no hope
I don't hang out with anyone
I don't respond to people
I try and get through shit on my own

But the last time I did that I ended up overdosing
So, if you're struggling right now
Don't be scared to ask for help
Don't be scared to tell the truth
I don't mean hang out with people every day
but check in with them
because sometimes you're allowed to
count on other people for happiness

One of my problems is
that I'm so used to being sad
I stop trying to be happy
Because being sad is comforting in a way
and when I'm happy I don't really know how to be
without listening to sad music
or wanting to watch a sad show

The stupid thing is, when all my friends hang out
and don't invite me because I always say no
my feelings get hurt
But in the end, it's my fault because
I never go anyway
Keep the friends close that invite you even when
they know it's going to be a no
I'm sorry to all the friends I lost because of it

My sadness is a backpack
It may not always be on my shoulders
but most of the time when I'm thinking too much
it's there

No matter where I am, it's there
My room, school, work
It's good to use for the times I need it
but it's been so heavy lately

I'm tired,
and I feel like no one can even see me

Loneliness: Feeling alone
It's not the fact of having no friends
because I do
It's that even in a room full of smiling people
one can feel so lonely
I think it's sad, really
Someone must have to be in a low, low state to
be that lonely
I'm not always in a low, low state, though
I'm just simply "lonely"

I am not upset you left
Everyone does
Good things must come to an end, you said
So thank you
I know it was hard being with someone so sad

but

Thank you for being the water to my flowers for
a few months
Thank you for making me smile when I could
no longer be happy
Thank you for filling the hole in my heart
for a while
I'm glad I met you

You healed my heart for a while
although in the end you left and the part of
my heart you put back together broke again
I am happy to say that you were whole,
you filled it
Thank you
Until we meet again

I have lots of friends
but I always still feel left out
They're great, they really are
I always like to include everyone,
because when I was a little girl,
I was the one excluded all the time
so now I never leave anyone alone to suffer

But how come it still happens to me?

No matter how good you are to people
No matter how sweet you may be or
how big your heart is

Some people don't give the kindness back
It will not always return to you

But that does not mean
You have to be an ass back
Because being kind brings you way farther in life
than being a douche
You just have to learn to accept that

Why do happy people make me so
mad sometimes?
Why can't I be happy?
Am I ever going to be?
I'm trying so hard to be

Fear: Something you're terribly scared of

Most people have a fear
Whether it be sharks, lions, roller coasters,
or thunderstorms
Everyone has a fear, it's impossible
not to have one

My fear is hurting people around me when I die

Dear therapist,

Thank you
Thank you for being a lifesaver at some point
in my life
Thank you for putting up with my attitude
on days I was sassy
And thank you for sometimes just sitting there
in silence with me
on days I don't speak a lot

I'm writing this one just as I left your office,
June 13, 2022
And I want you to know you saved a little girl's life
even if you annoy her with so many questions
sometimes
You helped her through times she felt lost
and she will always be grateful for that

I am healing
I am not healed
I am still in pain
But I'm trying to be the water for my own flowers

As you know, when you water flowers
after they seem broken
they don't bloom right away
It takes a while after being watered for them
to shine again

So hang in there
You'll bloom someday soon

What you see on the internet is not always real
In fact, it barely is, it's just a one-second proof
of a simple thing

Right now, I look like a gorilla
Like literally
But I don't care if I do
I'm telling you this

My hair looks like a bird's nest
I have sweat stains in my pits
I haven't brushed my teeth yet
I'm still wearing my pj's and it's late afternoon

But I'm cozy and comfortable
And that's what matters

People don't realize that, though
It's not about the amount of money you have
or
how pretty or popular you are
It's about how you treat yourself and others

It's about being who YOU are
not what others want you to be
It's okay if some days you are not doing anything
It's okay if some days you stay in your pj's
It's okay to not be perfect

Nobody is

Mom,

Thank you
Thank you for believing in me
when I couldn't myself
Thank you for supporting my every move
Thank you for having hope in me still
even if I don't myself
Most of all, thank you for being not only my mom
but also my best friend

I don't think I would have been able to do this
without you
I hope you know I love you very much, Mom
You are the strongest woman I've ever seen
and you inspire me to be every day

You are the water to my dying flowers
You are the sun to my plants
But mostly, you are my hero

There is nothing wrong with any of you
You are not hard to love
or difficult to deal with
You are not crazy
and you, especially, aren't unworthy

You are just a beautiful, broken soul
putting yourself back together

Bode,

Thank you
Thank you for keeping me active and working out
and for making sure I was always okay
Thank you for protecting me in times I was afraid
Thank you for being my father figure in times
I didn't have one

I hope you know
How proud of you I am
and how proud Dad would've been of you
You don't have to be afraid to share your
emotions anymore
Let them out

You are the lion in my life as a baby lion
You are the umbrella in my life of thundershowers
Mainly, you are my inspiration

I know it hurts
and I know it feels like your world is falling apart
and sometimes you just look forward
and see darkness
I know it's disturbingly hard to find happiness

But sometimes happiness
comes with the littlest things
like your morning coffee or
having a full pack of gum or
somebody telling you you're beautiful

But I want you to know that I need you
I know it feels like the end sometimes
but I promise you it's worth it to keep going

Wes,

Thank you
Thank you for always cheering me up
when I'm down
Thank you for bringing the light in me again
Thank you for being you

You are strong and fierce
And Dad would be so proud of how
you turned out, bud

You are the glow stick in my darkness
You are the smiley face in all my frowns
You are everything to me

If you're reading this right now

I hope you find your happiness someday
I hope you will live one day
I hope you find peace with yourself

Just know
I love you
And so does the world

Darc,

Thank you
Thank you for being my best friend
when I had none
Thank you for always sticking by my side
no matter what
Thank you for being my role model

I am so proud of you
Dad would be too
You are my lifesaver

You are the moon in my stars
You are the light at the end of my tunnel
You are the flower in my world of weeds
You are my person

I love you

To a simple quiet, but yet prominent, lovable
human being in my life ✺

I notice you
I know the world can be quite brutal toward you,
but you continue to get up each morning, and
show me what a strong soul is

Thank you for teaching me that it's okay
to be not okay
Thank you for allowing me to show
my true emotions in front of you
Thank you for making a lonely ghost soul
feel so seen
Thank you for not just not stepping on my
flowers, but for watering them with so much
nourishment you make them shine

You walked into my life when I needed
someone the most
and have helped me immensely since

I hope your flowers heal some day
from the people who walk all over them

You should give yourself the same love you give
to everyone else

Dad,

Thank you
Thank you for loving me those first twelve years
I had you
Thank you for making me feel confident
Thank you for being the best dad ever
You are not replaceable, and never will be

I miss you
I love you
But mostly,
I need you

You were the sunlight to my flowers
You were the everything I needed
And now you're gone

My angel

I know you're getting to the last few pages
But that doesn't mean it is the end

My journey has just begun
and so has yours
Although
I had to grow up too fast
there are many more flowers to grow . . .
there is a garden that could be filled

So
This is not going to be a sad ending
or a shocking one
or something that'll change you right away
or fix you
but I hope it makes you realize you're important
I want it to show you how strong you are
how amazing you can be

So when you feel like it's coming to an end
and you just cannot keep going
Plant some more seeds

(continued)

I am not always okay
And I am not 100 percent better

But I am able to say I'm functioning
I can get up and I can smile
I may not be fully happy
I may still have depression

But I am now able to get out of bed
I am now able to get out of bed
I am now able to get out of bed
I am now able to go through at least a week
without harming myself

It may still feel like your world is ending
some days
But I promise you it will get easier
Not necessarily all better
But easier

I am now proud to say
I am no longer scared of myself
I am no longer afraid of what I'll do to myself

I forgive myself
At times I still wish it would've worked
but at times I'm glad it didn't

I am now in control
I am now safe

My flowers are now living
At times they still need to be watered
because everybody needs a bit of help
sometimes
But for right now
for the first time
They're going to be okay

I believe you this time

Thank you to my mom Michelle, Bodie, Darcy,
and Wes
You are my heroes
and you are also my best friends
I am beyond lucky to have you
You are the lights in my world

Thank you to my extended family for
all the support and love you have for me
You helped me get through these rough times
each and everyone of you
I'm proud of you

Thank you to the sun in my life
You are incredible
You are worthy
You matter
Thank you for being my glow stick
Thank you for helping me shine again

Thank you to my best friend for sticking
by my side
Even when others left, you stayed
I am more than lucky to get to love you
You are my person

Thank you, too, all of you who have taught me
lessons in life

Thank you to those of you who have healed,
hurt, loved, and supported me
I'm glad I knew you for a while
I am not mad at those who have hurt me
But I thank you for making me a stronger human
each day

Make sure to check in with yourself
while reading this

The road may not always be an easy one,
but it will always be possible to drive on

At times it will be bumpy and
feel like a roller coaster

It's possible you might crash

But as long as you keep looking forward

You'll be fine

Just keep holding on . . .

www.ingramcontent.com/pod-product-compliance
Lightning Source LLC
Chambersburg PA
CBHW051633120626
46551CB00014B/2054